COLIN POWELL

By Geoffrey M. Horn

WORLD ALMANAC® LIBRARY

Please visit our web site at: www.worldalmanaclibrary.com
For a free color catalog describing World Almanac® Library's list
of high-quality books and multimedia programs, call 1-800-848-2928 (USA)
or 1-800-387-3178 (Canada). World Almanac® Library's fax: (414) 332-3567.

Library of Congress Cataloging-in-Publication Data

Horn, Geoffrey M.
    Colin Powell / by Geoffrey M. Horn.
      p. cm. — (Trailblazers of the modern world)
    Includes bibliographical references and index.
    ISBN 0-8368-5498-5 (lib. bdg.)
    ISBN 0-8368-5267-2 (softcover)
    1. Powell, Colin L.—Juvenile literature. 2. Statesmen—United States—Biography—Juvenile
literature. 3. Cabinet officers—United States—Biography—Juvenile literature. 4. Generals—
United States—Biography—Juvenile literature. 5. African American generals—Biography—
Juvenile literature. 6. United States. Army—Biography—Juvenile literature. I. Title.
II. Series.
   E840.8.P64H67   2004
   973.931'09—dc22
   [B]   2004047858

First published in 2005 by
World Almanac® Library
330 West Olive Street, Suite 100
Milwaukee, WI 53212 USA

Copyright © 2005 by World Almanac® Library.

Project manager: Jonny Brown
Editor: Jim Mezzanotte
Design and page production: Scott M. Krall
Photo research: Diane Laska-Swanke
Indexer: Walter Kronenberg

Photo credits: © Lucien Aigner/CORBIS: 13 top; © AP/Wide World Photos: cover; © Terry Ashe/Getty Images: 38 top;
© Ollie Atkins/White House/Time Life Pictures/Getty Images: 30; © Gabriel Benzur/Time Life Pictures/Getty
Images: 19 bottom; © Bettmann/CORBIS: 19 top, 25, 27, 33; © Dennis Brack/Mai/Mai/Time Life Pictures/Getty
Images: 5; © Jacques M. Chenet/CORBIS: 34; © Stephen Chernin/Getty Images: 42; © CORBIS SYGMA: 7, 8,
11 both, 13 bottom, 14, 23, 24, 29, 32; © Susan Farley/AFP/Getty Images: 9 bottom; © Louise Gubb/CORBIS: 4;
© Ronald S. Haeberle/Time Life Pictures/Getty Images: 28; © Stephen Jaffe/AFP/Getty Images: 41 bottom;
© Cynthia Johnson/Time Life Pictures/Getty Images: 40; © Steve Liss/Time Life Pictures/Getty Images: 9 top;
© Mansell/Time Life Pictures/Getty Images: 17; © Nilsen Alan Brian/CORBIS SYGMA: 41 top; © Ron
Sachs/CNP/CORBIS: 36; © Les Stone/CORBIS: 37; © Peter Turnley/CORBIS: 38 bottom; © U.S. Army/Time Life
Pictures/Getty Images: 26; © David H. Wells/CORBIS: 18; © James Whitmore/Time Life Pictures/Getty Images: 21

Printed in the United States of America

1 2 3 4 5 6 7 8 9 08 07 06 05 04

TABLE of CONTENTS

CHAPTER 1   SOLDIER AND STATESMAN   4

CHAPTER 2   JAMAICAN ROOTS   11

CHAPTER 3   WEARING THE UNIFORM   16

CHAPTER 4   LOVE AND WAR   21

CHAPTER 5   BEYOND VIETNAM   27

CHAPTER 6   FAST TRACK   31

CHAPTER 7   LINES IN THE SAND   37

TIMELINE   44

GLOSSARY   45

TO FIND OUT MORE   46

INDEX   47

Words that appear in the glossary are printed in **boldface**
type the first time they occur in the text.

CHAPTER 1

SOLDIER AND STATESMAN

Secretary of State Powell addresses a conference of world leaders in South Africa in 2002.

History was made at an elementary school near Crawford, Texas, on Saturday, December 16, 2000. On that day, President-elect George W. Bush named a retired general, Colin Powell, to become U.S. **secretary of state**.

Being chosen to direct the nation's foreign policy is a high honor. Many distinguished Americans have served in the president's **cabinet** as secretary of state. Leaders who have held that post include four of the nation's first six presidents—Thomas Jefferson, James Madison, James Monroe, and John Quincy Adams.

The event was historic for a different reason, however, as Powell, a proud African American, was quick to point out:

I would just like to note that in the newspaper stories that will be written about this occasion, they will say that Colin Powell was the first African-American to ever hold the position of secretary of state. And I'm glad they will say that. I want it repeated. I want it repeated because I hope it will give inspiration to young African-Americans coming along, but beyond that, all young Americans coming along—that no matter where you began in this society, with hard work and with dedication and with the opportunities that are presented by this society, there are no limitations upon you.

In announcing his choice for secretary of state, Bush noted that Powell had served in the U.S. Army for thirty-five years. Bush also pointed out that Powell had already been a trusted adviser to three U.S. presidents, "providing good counsel, strong leadership, and an example of integrity for everyone with whom he served." Bush concluded by saying that Powell was "an American hero, an American example, and a great American story."

Bush had another reason for choosing Powell. The presidential election on November 7, 2000, had been extremely close and ended in controversy. The outcome of the election hinged on Florida. Bush, a Republican, led by a few hundred votes in the state, but the Democrats demanded a recount. On December 12, the U. S. Supreme Court decided that the results in Florida could no longer be challenged, and Bush was declared the winner. Many people who had not voted for Bush were angry. They felt he did not really deserve to be president.

Four days later, when Bush stood with Powell in Crawford, he hoped that his choice of a new secretary of state would help heal the wounds from the election. Powell was already one of the most popular public figures in the United States. Many Americans who opposed Bush admired Powell. The U.S. Senate approved Bush's choice as soon as Bush became president in January 2001.

President Bush (center) and Powell's wife Alma joined the new secretary of state for his swearing-in ceremony in January of 2001.

How popular is Powell? When he was named secretary of state, 83 percent of Americans polled said they had a favorable view of him, and only 6 percent had an unfavorable opinion. He earned high marks from 90 percent of Republicans, 80 percent of Democrats, and 80 percent of independents. Three years later, after a difficult period as secretary of state, he was still admired by most Americans and by many other people throughout the world.

RISING THROUGH THE RANKS

A fellow officer once said that Powell would have succeeded "if he were green." Today, Powell enjoys so much

Powell's Popularity

Polls show that Colin Powell has consistently ranked as the most-admired member of President Bush's cabinet—more popular than the president and vice-president or any member of Congress. This table shows the results of several surveys taken to determine the popularity of U.S. politicians. The first survey was taken soon after September 11, 2001, when terrorists struck in the United States, and the last survey was taken in mid-December 2003, when U.S. forces captured former Iraqi dictator Saddam Hussein.

POSITVE RATINGS	Soon After 9/11	Feb. 2003	April 2003	Aug. 2003	Oct. 2003	Dec. 10–13	Dec. 14–16
President George Bush	88%	52%	70%	57%	59%	48%	50%
Secretary of State Colin Powell	88%	76%	81%	72%	70%	66%	74%
Vice President Dick Chaney	69%	45%	55%	42%	42%	36%	42%
Secretary of Defense Donald Rumsfeld	78%	56%	71%	55%	47%	47%	57%
Attorney General John Ashcroft	65%	51%	57%	48%	42%	41%	51%
House Speaker Dennis Hastert	52%	33%	41%	29%	29%	29%	24%
Republicans in Conogress	67%	43%	52%	41%	40%	34%	37%
Democrats in Congress	68%	38%	39%	30%	34%	30%	28%
Senate Majority Leader Bill Frist	NA	37%	39%	32%	29%	26%	28%

Source: The Harris Poll® #78, December 20, 2003

admiration and respect that it is easy to forget the many obstacles he and other black soldiers have had to overcome, before and during Powell's life-time. When Powell was born, in 1937, no African American had ever held the rank of general in the U.S. Army. Until the late 1940s, a policy of **segregation** in the U.S. Army kept most blacks separate from whites, and blacks had little chance to rise through the ranks.

The U.S. Army was not alone in providing few opportunities for African Americans. As late as 1960, no black person had ever been a member of a U.S. president's cab-inet or held a high policy-making position on the White House staff. To this day, no African American has ever been elected U.S. president. Powell seriously considered running for president in 1996 but decided against it.

During his three and a half decades as an active military man, Powell rose higher and faster than any other African American. He fought and was wounded in Vietnam, and he commanded troops in Germany and Korea. As a top White House adviser in the late 1980s, he helped to restore the reputation of the national security staff, which had been damaged by scandal.

From 1989 to 1993, Powell was chairman of the **Joint Chiefs of Staff**, the nation's highest military post. In that office, he helped to plan and carry out Operation Desert Storm, which forced Iraq to give up its occupation of Kuwait. Never before had an African American been given so much wartime responsibility.

In this 1954 photo, the seventeen-year-old Powell poses proudly in the uniform that he wore in the Reserve Officer Training Corps (ROTC).

When Powell took the oath of office as secretary of state in January 2001, he surely saw his appointment as the crowning moment of his career. Having spent so much of

With his wife Alma holding the Bible, Powell took the oath of office as chairman of the Joint Chiefs of Staff in 1989. Dick Cheney (left) was secretary of defense at that time and later became vice-president under George W. Bush.

his adult life practicing the art of war, he may have hoped that he would be able to devote his later years of government service to the pursuit of peace. History did not give him that opportunity.

Instead, Powell's time as secretary of state has been dominated by three conflicts. One conflict, still ongoing, has been the war against terrorism, including the hunt for members of **al-Qaeda**, the terrorist group that attacked targets in the United States on September 11, 2001. Another conflict took place in Afghanistan after September 11, when U.S. forces defeated the Taliban (the Islamic group ruling the country),

Colin Powell "Firsts"

Colin Powell is the first African American to serve as:

• Top national security adviser to the president
• Chairman of the Joint Chiefs of Staff
• Secretary of state

which had aided and protected al-Qaeda. The third conflict began in March 2003, when the United States and several of its allies invaded Iraq to remove Iraqi dictator Saddam Hussein from power.

Powell enjoys meeting with students, and he has headed a group dedicated to helping young people.

Many people in the United States and other parts of the world supported the use of U.S. troops in Afghanistan, as well as the U.S. war on terrorism, because the United States was acting in self-defense. Support for the invasion of Iraq, however, was not so widespread. Before the invasion, President Bush argued that Saddam posed a clear and serious danger to the United States and to the world. Many world leaders did not agree.

Some observers have wondered whether Powell was really in favor of a U.S. invasion of Iraq. If he had any doubts about the wisdom of going to war, however, he kept them private. In February 2003, Powell made the case against Saddam at the United Nations (UN). The following month, the United States, Britain, and a few other allies invaded Iraq. By mid-April, the government of Saddam Hussein was gone.

Today, the decision to attack and occupy

UN Secretary-General Kofi Annan shares a few words with Powell at a 2003 press conference on Middle East policy.

SECRETARY-GENERAL

Iraq remains controversial. The war will certainly affect historians' judgment of Powell. But even people who criticize him for his role in the Iraq conflict will find much to admire in his remarkable career as a soldier and statesman.

Colin Powell's Thirteen Rules

While serving as chairman of the Joint Chiefs of Staff, Powell became well known for keeping a list of thirteen rules to guide him in his daily decision making. He placed a list of these rules in plain view on his desktop and handed out copies to people who visited his office. Here are Powell's thirteen rules:

1. *It ain't as bad as you think. It will look better in the morning.*
2. *Get mad, then get over it.*
3. *Avoid having your ego so close to your position that when your position falls, your ego goes with it.*
4. *It can be done!*
5. *Be careful what you choose. You may get it.*
6. *Don't let adverse facts stand in the way of a good decision.*
7. *You can't make someone else's choices. You shouldn't let someone else make yours.*
8. *Check small things.*
9. *Share credit.*
10. *Remain calm. Be kind.*
11. *Have a vision. Be demanding.*
12. *Don't take counsel of your fears or naysayers.*
13. *Perpetual optimism is a force multiplier.*
[This last rule can also be stated as follows: If you always keep a positive attitude, you increase your own strength and the combined power of everyone who is working with you.]

Colin Luther Powell was born April 5, 1937, in the Harlem area of New York City. Both his parents were Jamaican immigrants. They had come separately to the United States in the early 1920s and had settled in New York, where they met and married. Their first child, Marilyn—Colin's older sister—was born in 1931.

Colin's father, Luther Theophilus Powell, was the second in a family of nine children. He grew up in a tiny, tin-roof shack in Top Hill, a rural area in southwestern Jamaica. Jobs were scarce on the island, so he hopped a banana boat to the United States, arriving in Philadelphia around 1920. He lacked a high school education, but he was able to find work as a gardener in Connecticut and as a building superintendent in New York City. Finally, he landed a job with a clothing firm in Manhattan's garment center, working his way up from stock clerk to shipping manager. His salary was low, but whenever he had a few extra dollars in his pocket, he enjoyed spending them on his children or helping neighbors in need.

The birth name of Colin's mother was Maud Ariel McKoy, but everyone knew her as Arie. The oldest of nine children, she was born in the Westmoreland region of Jamaica,

Luther Powell

"Arie" Powell

11

on the western end of the island. Unlike Luther, she finished high school, and while still living in Jamaica, she landed a job in a law office. Her mother, however, was unable to find work and left the island for the United States. In time she sent for Arie, who joined her in New York City. A firm in the garment center hired Arie to sew buttons and decorations on women's clothing.

A lifelong Democrat, Arie was a great admirer of Democratic U.S. president Franklin D. Roosevelt and a strong supporter of the International Ladies' Garment Workers Union. Luther, too, started out as a Democrat, but in 1952 he joined the majority of Americans who backed a Republican, Dwight Eisenhower, for president. Eisenhower, who was Supreme Allied Commander in Europe during World War II (1939–1945), found a home in the Republican Party after he retired from active duty, just as Colin Powell did several decades later.

How Do You Say Colin?

Do you know how to say Colin Powell's first name? Powell's family pronounces his name "Cah-lin," while most Americans think of him as "Coh-lin." In his **autobiography** *My American Journey*, Powell describes how he grew up hearing both pronunciations:

World War II changed my name. Before, I was Cah-lin, the British pronunciation that Jamaicans used. One of the first American heroes of the war was Colin P. Kelly, Jr. (pronounced Coh-lin). … Colin Kelly's name was on every boy's lips, and so, to my friends, I became Coh-lin of Kelly Street. To my family, I remain Cah-lin to this day. I once asked my father why he had chosen the name, which I never liked. Was it for some illustrious ancestor? Pop said no, he had read it off a shipping ticket the day I was born.

CITY BOY

When Colin was six years old, he moved with his parents and his older sister Marilyn to an apartment on Kelly

Street in the Hunts Point area of the South Bronx. In making the move from Harlem to Hunts Point, the Powells had relocated from a mostly black section of New York City to a racially mixed neighborhood. Jewish, Irish, Italian, Polish, Hispanic, and West Indian families lived within the same area. The West Indians there included a growing number of the Powells' Jamaican-born relatives.

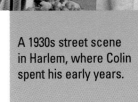

A 1930s street scene in Harlem, where Colin spent his early years.

Some of the happiest memories of Colin's childhood involved holiday get-togethers. Each New Years' Day, the family would gather at his Aunt Dot's home in Queens. The feast at her house included Jamaican favorites such as curried goat and Appleton Estate rum, and family members would sing the calypso (West Indian folk music) of their island homeland. Powell never lost his taste for calypso songs. After he became chairman of the Joint Chiefs of Staff, aides could hear him play calypso tapes in his office at the **Pentagon**.

This photo, showing Colin at about five years old, was probably taken in 1942, while the Powells were spending a summer Sunday with relatives in Queens.

HAPPY-GO-LUCKY

Colin was never a standout in school. In fourth grade, he was put in a class for slow learners. His parents wanted him to apply to Stuyvesant High School, one of the best high schools in New York City, but a guidance counselor told him not to bother. Instead, Colin went to Morris High School, a short walk from the Powells' Kelly Street apartment. At Morris, his grades remained unimpressive. He also did not show

"Those Cows Look Dangerous"

Colin Powell—a city boy who grew up in the Bronx—made no secret of his unfamiliarity with cattle ranching when he visited President-elect George W. Bush in Crawford, Texas, in December 2000. With Bush standing by his side, Powell joked with reporters and guests about how glad he was that the ceremony announcing his selection as secretary of state was not taking place on Bush's ranch:

I'm especially pleased that he chose to hold this ceremony in a school in Crawford, Texas. I was frankly glad it wasn't at the ranch. Nothing wrong with ranches, but I don't yet do ranch wear very well. And I'm from the South Bronx, and I don't care what you say: Those cows look dangerous.

great talent for music or sports. Powell later described himself as "a happy-go-lucky kid," who had ability but "lacked drive."

Although Colin got into mischief, he remained a good kid at heart. When he got caught, he admitted his mistakes and took responsibility for his actions. One

Colin and his older sister Marilyn stand in front of a Bronx apartment building, where the Powells lived for a brief period before moving to Kelly Street.

summer, for example, while he was attending church camp, he and some buddies sneaked out to buy beer. They hid their purchase in a toilet tank, where it was promptly discovered. The head priest did not accuse anyone, but instead called on the misbehaving campers to admit their guilt. Something in the priest's words awakened Colin's conscience, and he was the first to confess. "Your Colin stood up and took responsibility," his parents were told. "And his example spurred the other boys to admit their guilt."

Colin also earned a reputation as a willing worker. As a teenager, he worked part-time at Sickser's, a store in New York City that sold toys, baby carriages, and other items for children. Many of the customers at Sickser's were European Jews who spoke **Yiddish** as well as English. The little bits of Yiddish he picked up in those days still come in handy when Powell wants to charm Jewish audiences or an Israeli prime minister!

Staying Away from Drugs

While Colin was growing up, drugs and crime became major problems in the South Bronx. In a speech at Morris High School in 1991, Powell told students how he had managed to stay away from drugs:

We had lots of drugs in my neighborhood. On every street corner was some pothead or junkie who was trying to sell or deal or get others involved.

I didn't do it. Never in my life, not even to experiment, not to try, not to see what it would be like, for two reasons. One, my parents would have killed me, but the second reason is that somewhere along the line I and a couple of other of my friends ... knew it was stupid. It was stupid. It was the most self-destructive thing you could do with the life that God and your parents had given to you.

CHAPTER 3

WEARING THE UNIFORM

Colin Powell graduated from Morris High School after the fall 1953 semester. With a grade-point average of 78.3, his prospects were not particularly bright. Among Colin's family, however, there was no question that the sixteen-year-old would continue his education. "Our parents had these expectations that were kind of passed along to us," his older sister Marilyn recalled. "It was expected that we went to high school and after that we would go to college. They made us feel that education was the way to pull yourself up. Education was the key to success."

Powell applied to two local schools: New York University (NYU) and the City College of New York (CCNY). Both schools accepted him, but because CCNY's tuition was much less than NYU's, the choice was easy. When he enrolled at CCNY in 1954, he expected to major in engineering. ("That's where the money is," his mother told him.) He soon discovered, however, that he had absolutely no aptitude in that field, and he changed his major to geology. He liked studying rocks, but his heart was not really in his schoolwork.

FINDING A HOME IN THE ROTC

During his freshman year at City College, Powell was surprised to see hundreds of students wearing military uniforms. These students belonged to the Reserve Officer Training Corps (ROTC), a voluntary program run by the U.S. Army. Through ROTC, the Army provides money and training for college students.

Mop and Pop

In his autobiography, Powell describes how, as a college student, he spent one summer working as a porter (cleaning person) in a Pepsi-Cola bottling plant. The story shows the importance of doing the best you can, no matter how difficult or unpleasant the job.

The job was mine, though I was not quite sure what a porter did in a bottling plant. When I reported in, I was handed a mop, an experience that black workers have had for generations. I noticed that all the other porters were black and all the workers on the bottling machines were white. I took the mop. If that was what I had to do to earn $65 a week, I'd do it. I'd mop the place until it glowed in the dark. Whatever skill the job required, I soon mastered. You mop from side to side, not back and forth, unless you want to break your back. It could be godawful work, as it was the day fifty cases of Pepsi-Cola bottles came crashing down from a forklift and flooded the floor with sticky soda pop.

At the end of the summer, the foreman said, "Kid, you mop pretty good."

"You gave me plenty of opportunity to learn," I told him.

"Come back next summer," he said. "I'll have a job for you." Not behind a mop, I said. I wanted to work on the bottling machine. And the next year, that is where he put me. By the end of summer, I was deputy shift leader, and had learned a valuable lesson. All work is honorable. Always do your best, because someone is watching.

Lacking opportunity and education, generations of blacks were forced to take menial jobs such as shining shoes or mopping floors.

Today's ROTC programs give young people a head start in learning the technical, survival, and leadership skills a military career demands.

After graduation, ROTC members must serve as soldiers for several years.

Powell signed up for ROTC in the mid-1950s, at a time when most able-bodied young men expected to be drafted into the military. The advantage of ROTC was that graduates of the program could enter the Army as officers, while draftees would need to start on the bottom rung of the military ladder.

Powell was also attracted to ROTC for other reasons. "I liked the discipline and structure of the military," he told an interviewer. "I felt somewhat distinctive wearing a uniform. I hadn't been distinctive in much else." A boyhood friend remembered that Colin "used to love pacing up and down the block, practicing his marching, calling **cadence** out to himself. He thoroughly enjoyed it."

ROTC members were eligible to join one of the three military societies on the City College campus. Powell chose the Pershing Rifles, a group that took its name from a U.S. general, John Joseph Pershing (1860–1948). By the 1950s, the National Society of Pershing Rifles had more than 170 branches throughout the United States. Powell wrote that in the Pershing Rifles, or PRs, he found the close-knit group of friends he needed: "PRs drilled together. We partied together. We cut classes together. We chased girls together. ... The discipline, the structure, the **camaraderie**, the sense of belonging were what I craved."

Blacks in the Military

African Americans have a long tradition of combat service in the United States Army. Toward the end of the nineteenth century, however, the segregation of black soldiers from whites became increasingly common. After World War II, U.S. president Harry Truman decided to end racial segregation in the armed forces. On July 26, 1948, he issued Executive Order 9981, which stated that the military had to treat all members of the armed forces equally and fairly. This order made it possible for black officers such as Colin Powell to rise as high as their talents allowed.

Although Powell is the top-ranking African American in the history of the U.S. military, he was not the nation's first black general. In October 1940, President Franklin D. Roosevelt promoted Benjamin O. Davis, Sr. (1880–1970) to brigadier general, the highest rank attained by a black soldier up to that time.

Davis's son, Benjamin O. Davis, Jr. (1912–2002), was another important pioneer. He was the first African American in the twentieth century to graduate from the U.S. Military Academy at West Point. While he was there, he was shunned by his white classmates, who refused to chat with him or share meals with him. "Combat was not easy," he said, "but you could only get killed once. Living with the day-to-day degradation of racism was far more difficult."

During World War II, Davis commanded an all-black air unit, the famed Tuskegee Airmen. When he retired from the Air Force as a lieutenant general in 1970, he was the highest-ranking black officer in the U.S. military.

President Harry Truman ordered an end to racial segregation in the U.S. armed forces.

As a captain in 1942, Benjamin O. Davis, Jr. (far right) led the Tuskegee Airmen.

In June 1958, Powell graduated from City College and was commissioned as a second lieutenant in the U.S. Army. His next step was basic training at Fort Benning, Georgia. Army training was tough—a relentless ordeal of push-ups, sit-ups, marching, running, and hiking. When the trainees weren't exercising, they were taking classes, learning to handle their weapons, and sharpening their swamp, forest, and mountain survival skills. Powell, now twenty-one years old, thrived in this world and ranked among the best in his class.

The world outside Fort Benning was another matter. Fort Benning was located in the western part of Georgia, near the Alabama border, in the heart of the segregated South. In Columbus, a nearby town, blacks could shop at the local Woolworth's but were barred from sitting at the store's lunch counter. Water fountains and toilets were also segregated. Blacks and whites attended different churches, and a black man risked losing his life if he was caught flirting with a white woman.

The segregation and inequality Powell witnessed outside Fort Benning made him feel hurt and angry, but he was determined not to let his negative feelings affect his work. "I was not going to let myself become emotionally crippled," he later wrote. "I did not feel inferior, and I was not going to let anybody make me believe I was."

LOVE AND WAR

After finishing his training at Fort Benning, Powell was sent to the town of Gelnhausen in West Germany. Here he received his first command.

U.S. troops had been stationed in Germany since the end of World War II. When Powell arrived at Gelnhausen in October 1958, the **Cold War** between the United States and the **Soviet Union** was growing very intense. By then, Germany had been divided into **communist** East Germany and noncommunist West Germany. U.S. military planners feared that if the Cold War became "hot," huge numbers of Soviet tanks might roll into West Germany from the east, following a route U.S. officials called the Fulda Gap. If such an attack ever happened, the troops at Gelnhausen—which was not far from the Fulda Gap—would need to hold off the Soviet forces. The invasion ultimately never came, but U.S. troops had to be kept alert and combat ready, just in case.

During the late 1950s, the United States kept troops and weapons in West Germany to meet the threat of a Soviet invasion.

Force Structure

Colin Powell's first command in Germany was as a platoon leader in Company B, 2d Armored Rifle Battalion, 48th Infantry Regiment, 3d Armored Division. These terms reflect how the U.S. Army is organized. The Army's organization has changed somewhat since Powell first joined, but the basic form remains the same. Below is a simplified overview of the U.S. Army's structure today, with units listed from smallest to largest.

Squad
Number of soldiers: 9 or 10
Usually commanded by: sergeant

Platoon
Number of soldiers: 16 to 44
Usually commanded by: lieutenant
Includes: 2 to 4 squads

Company, Battery, or Troop
Number of soldiers: 62 to 190
Usually commanded by: captain
Includes: 3 to 5 platoons

Battalion or Squadron
Number of soldiers: 300 to 1,000
Usually commanded by:
  lieutenant colonel
Includes: 4 to 6 companies

Brigade, Regiment, or Group
Number of soldiers: 3,000 to 5,000
Usually commanded by: colonel
Includes: 2 to 5 battalions

Division
Number of soldiers: 10,000 to 15,000
Usually commanded by:
  major general
Includes: 3 brigades

Corps
Number of soldiers: 20,000 to 45,000
Usually commanded by:
  lieutenant general
Includes: 2 to 5 divisions

Army
Number of soldiers: 50,000 or more
Commanded by:
  lieutenant general or higher rank
Includes: 2 or more corps

COURTING ALMA

Powell spent two years in Germany, and during that time he was promoted to first lieutenant. He then returned to the United States. The Army assigned him to Fort Devens, in Massachusetts. The Devens posting changed Powell's life—though not in any way the Army could have expected.

In November 1961, a friend invited Powell to go double-dating. Colin's "blind date" for the evening was Alma Vivian Johnson. Born and raised in Birmingham, Alabama, Alma was a graduate of Fisk University in Nashville, Tennessee. She had come to Boston to study **audiology** and was currently working in a program to find and help people who were hard of hearing.

Colin and Alma took an immediate liking to each other and soon fell in love. "Alma Johnson was beautiful, intelligent, refined, and fun to be with, and, all too rare in a romance, she was my friend," he wrote later. "She came from a fine family, got along with my circle of friends, and was even a great cook. I knew that she loved me, and I loved her. My folks loved her too. ... Alma had everything I would ever want in a wife." They were married at the Congregational Church in Birmingham on August 25, 1962.

Not long after the wedding, Powell had to report to Fort Bragg, North Carolina, for additional training. With Christmas approaching, the Powells had much to celebrate. Alma was pregnant. Colin had been promoted to captain. Soon, he thought, he would have the opportunity to defend the cause of freedom in a faraway land. He had his orders. He was going to Vietnam.

Colin and Alma Powell were married in 1962 in Birmingham, Alabama. In this photo, Colin's parents stand to the left, and Alma's parents stand to the right.

Vietnam had once been a French colony. By the time Powell arrived for his first tour of duty (1962–1963), it had been divided into two separate, independent nations. North Vietnam had a communist government and was an ally of the Soviet Union. Its capital was in Hanoi. South Vietnam had a noncommunist government, and its capital was in Saigon.

This 1963 snapshot caught Powell—then a captain—in a relaxed moment at A Shau, South Vietnam.

South Vietnam was on the other side of the world from the United States, in Southeast Asia. It was a poor country with few resources, and any conflict there posed no direct threat to U.S. interests. So why did the United States send thousands of military advisers—and, later, hundreds of thousands of troops—to help defend South Vietnam? The answer has to do with the Cold War.

When communist rebels, backed by North Vietnam, tried to overthrow the South Vietnamese government, the government turned to the United States for help.

The Cold War was raging, and U.S. leaders were willing to send advisers, troops, weapons, and money to South Vietnam to oppose communism and stop the spread of Soviet influence.

Vietnam marked Powell's first direct encounter with the horror of combat. When asked to describe the most frightening experience of his life, he answered:

> *The first time somebody shot at me in Vietnam. I didn't get hit, but a soldier in the same patrol was killed, and I suddenly realized that this was no longer some training exercise or a game—it was for real. There were people out there on the other side of the war who were trying to kill me, and if they failed one day, they would try to kill me the next day. That was pretty scary to think about.*

Powell was wounded in July 1963, while serving as an adviser to South Vietnamese troops. He was walking on a jungle trail when he stepped into a trap—a hole dug and then concealed by the enemy. A bamboo spike hidden at the bottom of the hole pierced his foot, which rapidly became infected. For the injury, Powell received a medal—a Purple Heart. On his second tour of Vietnam (1968–1969), he was injured again.

More painful to Powell than any injury was the loss of many friends in Vietnam, including four of his college classmates. Between 1964 and 1973, nearly 60,000 U.S. soldiers died in Vietnam, and more than 150,000 were wounded. It is estimated that the war killed about 2 million Vietnamese and injured about 3 million. In 1973, the United States pulled its troops out of South Vietnam. Two years later, in 1975, Saigon fell to communist forces, and Vietnam became one country, ruled by a communist government.

In Vietnam, Powell learned that war was not a game. Instead, it was a terrifying experience in which real people could be wounded or killed.

A Daring Rescue

During Powell's second tour of duty in Vietnam, he showed great courage when a helicopter carrying him and several other officers crashed while trying to land in the hilly countryside west of Quang Ngai. In an interview three decades later, Powell described the terrifying scene:

I could see that it was a difficult mission, and I realized that [the pilot] was starting—I could see the ground, see the trees, and watch the pilot—and I realized he was starting to lose a little control. Then suddenly [the helicopter] shifted left about three feet, and I'll never forget watching the blade hit the tree, and it stopped instantly. And once a blade stops instantly in a helicopter, it is no longer flying. It is a rock. We essentially just went down like an elevator without a cable. … I bent over, put my hands under my knees, and waited for it to hit.

It hit, and there was a huge crash, and I don't think you think about anything but leaving, so I just hit the belt and jumped and ran away for a few feet, turned around and looked, and realized it was starting to smoke now, and I ran back and got the [commanding general] out. … Your values and your training and then your instinct just goes to work. Nothing's conscious.

During the next few moments, Powell helped pull other survivors from the smoking wreckage. Not until he was X-rayed at a hospital later that day did he realize the extent of his own injuries. He had rescued the others by running back and forth on a broken ankle!

After a helicopter crash in 1968 near Quang Ngai, Powell (right) showed his courage by carrying several of his fellow officers to safety.

When Powell returned home to the United States in 1969 after his second tour of duty in Vietnam, the country was bitterly divided over the war. Like many other U.S. soldiers who went to Vietnam, Powell was angry about the way the war had been fought. He objected to the fact that many "poorer, less educated, less privileged" young men had been sent to fight in Vietnam, while most "sons of the powerful and well placed" had found ways to avoid serving overseas.

In his book *My American Journey*, Powell makes clear exactly where he thinks the United States went wrong in Vietnam:

In the late 1960s, many college campuses in the United States became hotbeds of protest against the Vietnam War.

> *When we go to war, we should have a purpose that our people understand and support; we should mobilize the country's resources to fulfill that mission and then go in to win. In Vietnam, we had entered into a halfhearted half-war, with much of the nation opposed or indifferent, while a small fraction carried the burden. ... Many of my generation, the career captains, majors, and lieutenant colonels seasoned in that war, vowed that when our turn came to call the shots, we would not quietly **acquiesce** in halfhearted warfare for half-baked reasons that the American people could not understand or support.*

Murder at My Lai

In March 1968, in a South Vietnamese village called My Lai, U.S. soldiers led by First Lieutenant William Calley killed 347 Vietnamese civilians. Many of the victims were old men, women, and children. The killings, carried out by members of the 11th Brigade of the American Division, became known as the My Lai massacre.

Months after the massacre, Powell—who had been promoted to major—became the American Division's chief staff officer for operations and planning. This job made him the keeper of the division's journal of operations—which contained evidence of the "kills" reported by Calley's platoon.

No one has ever accused Powell of having anything to do with the My Lai killings. He was not even in Vietnam when they took place. Some writers have criticized him, however, for not acting to uncover the My Lai massacre, which did not come to light until late in 1969.

Victims of the My Lai massacre in 1968

By the end of the 1960s, Powell's combat days were over. He was a married man in his early thirties, with a growing family to support. At that point, Powell had combat medals and military savvy. If he was going to reach the top as a career Army officer, however, he would also need to broaden his education and hone his political know-how.

Powell had not been a great student in high school or college, but he understood the career value of sharpening his classroom skills. During 1967 and 1968, between his tours of duty in Vietnam, he had studied at the Army Command and General Staff College, at Fort Leavenworth, Kansas. Powell already knew what war looked, smelled, and felt like at ground level. At Leavenworth, he gained a deeper understanding of what was involved in training, feeding, supplying, and moving a division of more than ten thousand soldiers and using them effectively in combat.

Powell returned to the academic world in the autumn of 1969, enrolling in a master's degree program at George Washington University, in Washington, D.C. He studied math, economics, statistics, and computer science. Both on and off campus, growing numbers of people were protesting the Vietnam War. "It was an odd sensation," he wrote, "passing by fraternity houses where sheets painted with the peace symbol and antiwar slogans fluttered from windows and soapbox **orators** condemned the war I had fought in."

The Army, which promoted Powell to lieutenant colonel in 1970, allowed him two full years to complete his course work. In 1971, he received an M.B.A (master's degree in business administration) in data processing. In the meantime, the Powell family had settled in the Washington, D.C., area, where they would remain for most of the next three decades.

The Powells in 1975. From left to right, the three Powell children are Annemarie, Linda, and Michael.

The Powell Family

Colin and Alma Powell celebrated their fortieth wedding anniversary in August 2002. They have three children: Michael (born 1963), Linda (born 1965), and Annemarie (born 1970). Like his father, Michael is an influential figure in Washington, D.C. President Bill Clinton appointed him to the Federal Communications Commission (FCC) in 1997. Four years later, President George W. Bush promoted him to chairman of the FCC. Linda, an actress, has appeared on stage, in movies, and on television.

WHITE HOUSE FELLOW

In the fall of 1971, while Powell was working at the Pentagon, he was encouraged to apply for a White House fellowship. The purpose of the White House fellowship program was to give a small group of talented young men and women an opportunity to experience what it was like to work at the highest levels of the United States government. Selection was very competitive, and Powell was one of only seventeen fellows chosen for 1972–1973.

The group met regularly throughout the year, and Powell quickly emerged as a leader. "He was older," another fellowship winner recalled. "He had more experience than most of us. He helped people with the perspective of what was important and what was not. He was a nice guy, a bright one, a **consensus** builder. All the things people write about him now, they were there then."

Asked to choose which government agency he wanted to work for, Powell picked the Office of Management and Budget, or OMB. The OMB prepares the president's detailed annual budget request to Congress. It is one of the most powerful government agencies in Washington, playing a major role in deciding how much money other agencies and departments receive.

Richard M. Nixon (left) was U.S. president when Powell became a White House fellow in 1972.

The work Powell did at OMB was not as important as the people he met there. The budget director was Caspar Weinberger, who got the nickname "Cap the Knife" because of his eagerness to cut costs. Weinberger's top assistant was Frank Carlucci. "You gave him a project, it got done," Carlucci said of Powell in 2001. "It was easy to spot him as a rising talent." Both men would play important roles in Powell's future.

FAST TRACK

Powell covered a lot of ground during the 1970s. After completing his White House fellowship, he requested and received an assignment in South Korea. During the Korean War, in the early 1950s, the United States and other countries defended noncommunist South Korea against an invasion by communist North Korea. Tens of thousands of U.S. troops have been stationed in South Korea ever since, guarding the cease-fire line between the two countries. In South Korea, Powell served as a battalion commander.

Although Powell hated the separation from his wife Alma and their children, being away from Washington during 1973–1974 was an excellent career move. When Powell left for South Korea, Richard M. Nixon was U. S. president, and the White House was engulfed in the Watergate scandal. By the time Powell returned to the Pentagon in 1974, President Nixon had been forced to resign, and the worst of the scandal was over.

During 1975–1976, Powell was back in the classroom as a student at the National War College. Located in the Washington area at Fort McNair, the National War College was an elite school—"the Harvard of military education," as Powell called it. The advanced courses included the works of history's greatest military thinkers. Powell did well, and his classmates had little doubt that he was on his way to the top.

A promotion to full colonel came through in February 1976. As soon as his War College studies were finished, Powell was off to Fort Campbell, Kentucky, where he took command of the 2d Brigade of the 101st Airborne Division (the "Screaming Eagles").

Promoted to colonel in 1976, Powell led the 2d Brigade of the 101st Airborne Division at Fort Campbell, Kentucky.

Three years later, Powell received another huge career boost—promotion to brigadier general. The June 1979 ceremony awarding him his general's star prompted a huge family celebration. Powell felt special pride in having his mother Arie at the event, which took place in the dining room of the secretary of defense. "Mom was as nervous as a bride," he wrote, "constantly bugging Alma to help her fix her hair, iron her dress, and approve her wardrobe until you would think she was getting the star." Powell's only regret was that his father, who had died in 1978, did not live long enough to see him become a general.

POLITICAL GENERAL

While continuing to rise through the ranks of the military, Powell held a series of political posts under two very different presidents: Jimmy Carter, a Democrat from Georgia, and Ronald Reagan, a Republican

A Rapid Rise

During his military career, Colin Powell moved quickly up the Army chain of command. Below are the dates of some of the important promotions he received, from the time he was commissioned as a second lieutenant in 1958 to his retirement from the military in 1993.

1959	First lieutenant
1962	Captain
1966	Major
1970	Lieutenant colonel
1976	Colonel
1979	Brigadier general
1983	Major general
1986	Lieutenant general
1989	General and chairman of the Joint Chiefs of Staff

from California. During the late 1970s, under President Carter, Powell served briefly in the Department of Energy and then, from 1979 to 1981, as senior military aide to the deputy secretary of defense.

Powell spent the next two years on bases at Fort Carson, Colorado, and Fort Leavenworth, Kansas. Then, in 1983, with Reagan now U.S. president, Powell was summoned back to Washington, D.C. Caspar Weinberger—Powell's boss at the Office of Management and Budget, when Powell was a White House fellow—had become secretary of defense, and he wanted Powell to be his top military aide.

The moving around that Powell's career demanded took a serious toll on his family, and his teenage daughter Linda was becoming particularly upset. Powell did not really want to come back to the Pentagon, but there was no way he could reject Weinberger's offer without hurting his own career.

Other changes came to the Powell family in the mid-1980s. Alma's father, a widower for twelve years, died in February 1984. Colin's mother died four months later.

Powell was serving as a top military aide at the Pentagon when U.S. combat troops landed on the Caribbean island of Grenada in 1983.

Buffalo Soldiers

While Powell was at Fort Leavenworth, Kansas, in the early 1980s, he became interested in the history of four African American regiments that Congress had created after the Civil War. Called "Buffalo Soldiers" by Native American warriors who clashed with them, members of these regiments helped settle the West and played important roles in several conflicts. Although the African Americans in these regiments proved themselves to be excellent soldiers and won many medals, they had never received proper recognition. Powell was outraged that Leavenworth, which had monuments to many military heroes, remembered the all-black regiments with only a couple of "dirt roads in an abandoned trailer park."

Powell began campaigning for a statue to honor the brave African Americans who had served in these regiments. Through his efforts, a memorial to the Buffalo Soldiers was completed in 1992.

Veterans of an all-black Army unit saluted the achievements of the Buffalo Soldiers at a meeting with Powell (far right) in Detroit, Michigan, in 1995.

THE BUFFALO SOLDIERS

POWELL

During the mid-1980s, when Powell was working for Weinberger, the secretary of defense learned of a complicated scheme hatched by some members of President Reagan's national security staff. At this time, Iran—an enemy of the United States—was involved in a long, bloody war with its Middle East neighbor, Iraq. Iran desperately needed weapons. The national security staffers decided that the United States should secretly sell missiles to Iran. In return, Iran agreed to use its influence to try to free several Americans who were being held hostage in a third Middle East country, Lebanon.

Selling arms to Iran was against U.S. policy—and so was trading weapons for hostages. Weinberger, Powell, and others in the Department of Defense knew about the plan and tried to stop it, but President Reagan approved it anyway. Weinberger then had Powell arrange to have the missiles shipped to Iran.

At the same time, the national security staff faced a problem in Central America. Reagan and his top advisers did not like the government of Nicaragua, which they believed was pro-communist. The national security staffers wanted to provide assistance to a rebel group, known as the Contras, that was trying to overthrow the Nicaraguan government. Congress opposed this assistance and voted to stop the flow of U.S. funds to the Contras. To get around Congress, the national security staff used money from the Iran arms sales—plus other secret funds—to help the Contra rebels.

This unwise and illegal scheme unraveled in late 1986. The scandal left the White House in turmoil and the national security staff in disgrace. To clean up the mess, Reagan named Frank Carlucci—another former Powell boss—as his top national security adviser.

Carlucci then asked Powell to become his deputy. Together, the two men reorganized the National Security Council and restored its good name.

The following year, Carlucci succeeded Weinberger as secretary of defense, allowing Powell to take another giant step up the Washington career ladder. For the very first time, an African American held the title of assistant to the president for national security affairs. Powell—the child from Harlem and Hunts Point, a proud son of Jamaican immigrants—had entered the inner circle of U.S. presidential power.

CHAPTER 7

The victory of George Herbert Walker Bush in the 1988 presidential election brought another big boost for Powell's career. Bush—who had spent eight years as Ronald Reagan's vice president—announced in August 1989 that he wanted Powell to become chairman of the Joint Chiefs of Staff. Powell was not only the first African American to hold the office. He was also, at fifty-two years of age, the youngest person ever to have that responsibility.

At the time, the world was changing rapidly. The Soviet Union's communist empire was beginning to crumble, and Eastern European countries were throwing off communist rule one by one. Nowhere, however, were developments more changeable and challenging than in the Middle East.

In 1989, after Powell had become chairman of the Joint Chiefs of Staff, U.S. president George H. W. Bush ordered U.S. troops to invade Panama and arrest the country's dictator, Manuel Noriega. Noriega was accused of drug trafficking.

WAR IN THE MIDDLE EAST

The Middle East region looms large in U.S. foreign policy. It is the birthplace of three religions—Judaism, Christianity, and Islam. It also provides most of the world's oil, which is used to make fuel and other necessities. Without a steady supply of oil, modern life would stop dead in its tracks.

For this reason, alarm bells went off in Washington when Iraqi dictator Saddam Hussein invaded Kuwait in

Displaying a map of the Middle East, Powell briefed the press about Iraq's takeover of Kuwait in August 1990.

Retreating Iraqi troops set fire to Kuwait's oil wells in February 1991.

August 1990. Because both Iraq and Kuwait have huge oil deposits, the conquest gave Saddam control over a large share of the world's oil. The takeover of Kuwait also left Saddam in position to threaten another oil-rich neighbor, Saudi Arabia, a longtime U.S. ally.

President Bush decided it was time to draw a "line in the sand." With authorization from the UN, the U.S. military led a coalition of UN forces in Operation Desert Storm, a large-scale effort to drive the Iraqis out of Kuwait. The resulting conflict, called the Persian Gulf War, tested the leadership skills of three men: Powell, Secretary of Defense Dick Cheney, and Desert Storm commander H. Norman Schwarzkopf. The Gulf War also allowed Powell to test the ideas of his "Powell Doctrine," a set of guidelines for the use of U.S. military force.

The war went extraordinarily well. In little more than six weeks, Saddam was forced to give up Kuwait. The combat devastated Iraq's best fighting force but killed fewer than 150 U.S. soldiers. Powell shared in the success. He was acclaimed a hero for the nation and a role model for African Americans.

What the war did not do was remove Saddam from power. Powell defended the decision by the United States and its allies not to roll on to Baghdad, the Iraqi capital. What purpose would have been served, he wrote in 1992, if allied forces had tried to capture Saddam? "And would serving that purpose have been worth the many more casualties that would have occurred? Would it have been worth the

The Powell Doctrine

In an article that appeared in *Foreign Affairs* magazine in 1992, Powell listed some questions that political leaders in the United States needed to ask before committing the country to war. Here, in simplified form, are some of those questions:

- Are the war's goals important, clearly defined, and clearly understood?
- Have all nonviolent means of achieving those goals failed?
- Will military force achieve those goals? At what cost?
- Do the possible gains outweigh the risks?

Powell's ideas about war developed out of his experiences in Vietnam. His views have come to be known as the Powell Doctrine. According to the Powell Doctrine:

- War should be used only as a last resort.
- When going to war, the United States needs, from the very beginning, to commit enough force to overwhelm the enemy.
- The public must strongly support military action and understand why it is necessary.
- Planners must have an exit strategy—a reasonably clear view of how the war will end and when the troops can come home.

inevitable follow-up: major occupation forces in Iraq for years to come ... ?" Powell's answer was no. A decade later, he would have reason to reconsider those remarks.

CIVILIAN LIFE

Powell had served two Republican presidents, Reagan and Bush, and had held two of the highest positions in the United States government. The nation was ready for change, however, and so was Powell. In 1993, a Democrat, Bill Clinton, became U.S. president. By the fall of 1993, Powell had given up his Joint Chiefs

Colin and Alma Powell at a ceremony honoring Powell's retirement from the military

chairmanship. After thirty-five years in the military, he had decided to hang up his uniform.

After returning to civilian life, Powell worked on his autobiography, which became a best-seller. He flirted with the idea of running for president, and in November 1995, he held a press conference at which he declared himself a Republican. At the same time, however, he told reporters that he would not be a candidate for either the presidency or the vice presidency in 1996. Powell said that he had looked deep into his own soul and found that he did not have the "passion and commitment" that a long campaign would require. Political writers noted that some **conservatives** had vowed to oppose Powell because they objected to his moderate views on issues such as race, abortion, gun control, and welfare.

In 1997, Powell took part in the Presidents' Summit for America's Future. This meeting, which included President Clinton and other current and former national leaders, focused on various ways to help the nation's young peo-

Gays in the Military

When Bill Clinton ran for president in 1992, he pledged to allow openly gay men and women to serve in the military. Homosexuals have long served in the U.S. armed forces. Over the years, however, many gays have been harassed by fellow soldiers and discharged from service.

Powell was in his final months as chairman of the Joint Chiefs of Staff when Clinton took office in January 1993. Powell publicly opposed the Clinton policy. He argued that allowing openly gay men and women to serve would be bad for discipline and morale. Instead, he agreed to support a different policy—"Don't ask, don't tell, don't pursue." This policy means that gays can serve in the military if they keep quiet about their sexual orientation, but they can still be dismissed if their homosexuality becomes public knowledge.

Many people thought Powell was absolutely right, but others disagreed. How, his critics asked, could a champion of equal opportunity for blacks in the military deny gays the same chance to defend the nation?

ple. The conference resulted in the creation of America's Promise— The Alliance for Youth. This group includes more than 400 different organizations that have pledged to operate or support youth programs throughout the United States. Powell headed America's Promise until he was picked to become secretary of state in December 2000.

Volunteer projects took much of Powell's time in the late 1990s.

BACK TO IRAQ

The election of George W. Bush—the son of the president who had made Powell chairman of the Joint Chiefs— brought many familiar faces back to the White House. Dick Cheney, the former secretary of defense, was now vice president. Like Powell, Cheney had been deeply involved in the 1991 war against Saddam Hussein.

As secretary of state, Powell began dealing with dozens of trouble spots throughout the world. He also had to face continuing threats from al-Qaeda terrorists. From 2002 onward, however, President Bush and his advisers focused increasingly on Iraq. They suspected that Saddam Hussein was developing, building, and stockpiling nuclear, chemical, and biological weapons. They insisted that Saddam had to be stopped before he used these weapons against his neighbors or gave them to terrorist groups for use against the United States.

On February 5, 2003, Powell went to the United Nations to lay out the United States' case against Saddam. He gave a powerful speech, and because he had a reputation for honesty and

Three key leaders of the Iraq war in 2003: President George W. Bush (left), National Security Adviser Condoleezza Rice, and Secretary of Defense Donald Rumsfeld.

integrity, many people believed him. Powell spoke in great detail for ninety minutes. He said he had evidence to prove, beyond any doubt, that Saddam posed a danger to the rest of the world. He also said that if the United Nations did not join the United States in taking action against Iraq, the United States was prepared to act alone.

Despite Powell's speech, the UN did not agree to an invasion of Iraq, and several longtime U.S. allies—including France and Germany—refused to join the United States in taking action against Saddam. Nonetheless, in March of 2003, the United States, Britain, and a few other allies invaded Iraq. Within three weeks, the government of Iraq collapsed. Saddam fled Baghdad and hid for more than eight months, but he was captured by U.S. troops in December.

Powell's job as secretary of state required him publicly to support and defend President Bush's policies—even those with which he may privately have disagreed.

POWELL'S LEGACY

Saddam is a cruel man who killed hundreds of thousands of people. Many Iraqis were happy to be rid of him. But when U.S. troops occupied the country and inspectors began looking for the weapons Bush, Cheney, and Powell had warned against, they found nothing. After nearly a year of searching, inspectors concluded that much of what Powell had said at the United Nations was not true. Had Powell been misled? Did the United States go to war based on faulty information?

Historians may someday determine whether Powell disagreed with going to war. They may also study the plans made for the postwar occupation of Iraq. Was the war really necessary? Did the Pentagon send enough troops to accomplish its mission, and were the troops trained and equipped properly? Did the gains outweigh the risks? Was there a carefully planned exit strategy? These questions are part of the Powell Doctrine, which Powell established to avoid the mistakes made in Vietnam. Did Powell raise any of these concerns with President Bush and other U.S. leaders before or during the war? It may take years for the answers to be known.

Powell had surgery for prostate cancer in December 2003 but appeared to make a vigorous recovery. The following April, he celebrated his sixty-seventh birthday. Whatever the future may hold—and however painful his recent experiences may have been—Colin Powell is likely to seek new ways to serve the nation he loves. "Our responsibility as lucky Americans," he wrote, "is to try to give back to this country as much as it has given to us, as we continue our American journey together."

Awards and Honors

Colin Powell has been honored many times in his life. For his service in Vietnam, he was awarded two Purple Hearts, a Bronze Star, the Soldier's Medal, and the Legion of Merit. He has twice received the nation's highest civilian honor, the Presidential Medal of Freedom. President George H. W. Bush awarded the medal to Powell in 1991, and President Bill Clinton awarded the medal to him again in 1993.

After the Gulf War, Powell received the Congressional Gold Medal, awarded by an act of Congress. Powell's other honors include an honorary knighthood, received in 1993 from Britain's Queen Elizabeth II.

1937	Colin Luther Powell is born April 5 in New York City
1948	U.S. president Harry Truman issues executive order on July 26, ending segregation in the U.S. armed forces
1958	Powell graduates from City College of New York, is commissioned as second lieutenant in U.S. Army, and gets his first command at Gelnhausen, Germany
1962	Marries Alma Vivian Johnson, August 25
1963	On his first tour of duty in Vietnam, Powell is wounded when he steps into an enemy trap
1968	On his second tour of duty in Vietnam, Powell saves several officers in a helicopter crash
1971	Earns master's degree from George Washington University
1972–1973	As a White House fellow, works at Office of Management and Budget
1975–1976	Studies at National War College
1983–1986	Assistant to Secretary of Defense Caspar Weinberger
1987–1989	National security adviser to President Ronald Reagan
1989–1993	Chairman of the Joint Chiefs of Staff
1991	During Operation Desert Storm, a coalition led by the United States forces Iraq to give up Kuwait
1993	Powell retires from the military
1995	*My American Journey* published
1997	America's Promise—The Alliance for Youth founded
2000	President George W. Bush names Powell as secretary of state, December 16
2001	Al-Qaeda launches terrorist attacks against the United States, September 11
2003	At the United Nations on February 5, Powell makes the case for war against Iraq; a military invasion led by the United States ousts Iraqi dictator Saddam Hussein in April; Powell has cancer surgery, December 15

acquiesce: accept without protest.

al-Qaeda: "the Base" in Arabic, an international terrorist network founded by Osama bin Laden in the late 1980s.

audiology: the scientific study of hearing.

autobiography: an account of a person's life written by that person.

cabinet: in the U.S. government, a group of advisers to the president, consisting of the heads of the major federal government departments.

cadence: during a military drill, the series of commands a leader calls out to keep a group marching in step.

camaraderie: friendship or goodwill.

Cold War: a rivalry between the United States and the Soviet Union, as well as their respective allies, that lasted from 1945 to 1991.

communist: having to do with a political system in which the government owns most or all property and controls the economy. The system often involves one party holding absolute power.

consensus: agreement by all.

conservatives: people who seek to preserve traditional views and values and often oppose social change.

Joint Chiefs of Staff: the heads of the U.S. Army, Navy, Air Force, and Marine Corps, led by a chairman selected from one of the armed services.

orators: people making speeches.

Pentagon: the headquarters of the U.S. Department of Defense, named after the five-sided building that contains it.

secretary of state: in the U.S. government, the cabinet official who heads the State Department and directs the nation's foreign policy.

segregation: the policy or practice of requiring people of different races or backgrounds to use separate facilities.

Soviet Union: a communist nation that consisted of Russia and neighboring republics and existed from 1922 to 1991.

Yiddish: a language originally spoken by Jews in Central and Eastern Europe.

BOOKS

Finlayson, Reggie. *Colin Powell (Biography)*. Minneapolis: Lerner Publications, 2004.

Flanagan, Alice K. *Colin Powell: U.S. General and Secretary of State*. Chicago: Ferguson, 2001.

Horn, Geoffrey M. *The Armed Forces (World Almanac Library of American Government)*. Milwaukee: World Almanac Library, 2003.

Powell, Colin L., with Joseph E. Persico. *My American Journey*. New York: Ballantine Books, 2003.

Shaw, Lisa (ed.). *In His Own Words: Colin Powell*. New York: Perigee, 1995.

Strong, Mike. *Colin Powell: It Can Be Done! (High Five Reading)*. Mankato, Minn.: Capstone, 2003.

Waxman, Laura Hamilton. *Colin Powell (History Maker Bios)*. Minneapolis: Lerner Publications, 2005.

Wheeler, Jill C. *Colin Powell (Breaking Barriers)*. Edina, Minn.: Abdo & Daughters, 2002.

INTERNET SITES

Academy of Achievement
www.achievement.org/autodoc/page/pow0int-1
Includes a biography and an interview.

America's Promise
www.americaspromise.org/
Official site of the organization founded by Powell.

DefenseLINK
www.defenselink.mil/
Official site of the United States Department of Defense.

NPR: Colin Powell
www.npr.org/news/specials/cpowell/
National Public Radio site includes Powell's speech about Iraq to the UN in 2003.

U.S. Department of State
http://state.gov/
The State Department's official web site.

Page numbers in *italics* indicate illustrations.

Adams, John Quincy, 4
Afghanistan, 8–9
African-Americans *see* Black Americans
al-Qaeda (terrorist organization), 8–9, 41
America's Promise--The Alliance for Youth, 41
Annan, Kofi, *9*
Army, U.S.
  basic training, 20
  desegregation of, 7, 19
  modern structure, 22
  ROTC program, 16, 18
Army Command and General Staff College, 28
Ashcroft, John, 6

Birmingham, Alabama, 23, *23*
Black Americans
  limited job opportunities for, 17, *17*
  Powell firsts, 4, 7, 8
  in U.S. cabinet, 7
  in U.S. military, 7, 19, *19*, 34, *34*
  as victims of segregation in South, 20
Buffalo Soldiers, 34, *34*
Bush, George Herbert Walker, 37, 39, 43
Bush, George W., 4–6, *5*, 14, 29, *41*, 41–42

Calley, William, 28
calypso, 13
Carlucci, Frank, 30, 35–36, *36*
Carter, Jimmy, 32–33
Cheney, Dick, 6, *8*, 38, 42
City College of New York (CCNY), 16, 18, 20
Civil War, U.S. (1861-65), 34
Clinton, Bill, 29, 39, 40, 43
Cold War, 21, 24-25
Congressional Gold Medal, 43

Contras (Nicaraguan rebels) *see* Iran-Contra affair

Davis Jr., Benjamin O., 19, *19*
Davis Sr., Benjamin O., 19
Democratic Party, 5, 6, 12

Eisenhower, Dwight D., 12
Elizabeth II, Queen (Great Britain), 43

Federal Communications Commission, 29
Fisk University, 23
Foreign Affairs (magazine), 39
Fort Benning (Georgia), 20
Fort Bragg (North Carolina), 23
Fort Campbell (Kentucky), 31, *32*
Fort Carson (Colorado), 33
Fort Devens (Massachusetts), 23
Fort Leavenworth (Kansas), 28, 33, 34
Fort McNair (Washington, D.C), 31
France, 42
Frist, Bill, 6

gays in the military, 40
George Washington University, 29
Germany, 42 *see* also West Germany
Great Britain, 42, 43
Grenada, *33*
Gulf War *see* Persian Gulf War

Hastert, Dennis, 6
homosexuality *see* gays in the military
Hussein, Saddam, 6, 9, 37–38, 41–42

International Ladies' Garment Workers Union, 12
Iran-Contra affair, 35–36
Iraq, 7, 9–10, 37–39, *38*, *41*, 41–43

Jamaica, 11, 13
Jefferson, Thomas, 4

Joint Chiefs of Staff, 7, 37

Kelly Jr., Colin P., 12
Korean War (1950-53), 31
Kuwait, 7, 37–38, 38

Lebanon, 35

Madison, James, 4
Monroe, James, 4
Morris High School, 13–16
My American Journey (Powell autobiography), 12, 27, 40
My Lai massacre, 28, *28*

National Security Council, 36
National War College, 31
New York City
  Powell Bronx upbringing, 12–15
  Powell Harlem roots, 11, 13, *13*
Nicaragua, 35
Nixon, Richard M., *30*, 31
Noriega, Manuel, 37

Office of Management and Budget (OMB), 30, 33
Operation Desert Storm, 7, 38

Panama, *37*
Pepsi-Cola Bottling Co., 17
Pershing, John Joseph, 18
Pershing Rifles, National Society of, 18
Persian Gulf War, 38, 43
Powell, Alma Vivian Johnson (wife), *5*, *8*, 23, *23*, 29, *29*, 31, 32, 33, *40*
Powell, Annemarie (daughter), 29, *29*
Powell, Arie (Maud Ariel McKoy) (mother), *11*, 11–12, 32, 33
Powell, Colin
  awards and honors, 43
  basic training undergone by, 20
  Buffalo Soldiers recognition campaign, 34, *34*
  cancer surgery, 43

as college student, 16–18, 20
family background, 11–12
first name pronounced two
    ways, 12
at Fort Campbell, 31, *32*
as Joint Chiefs of Staff
    chairman, 7, 8, *8*, 10, 13,
    37, 39, 40-41
master's degree earned by, 29
military career surveyed, 7, 32
as national security adviser, 8,
    36, *36*
New York childhood, 11–15,
    13, 14
Persian Gulf War role, 38, *38*
presidential candidacy mulled,
    7, 40
public opinion of, 6
retirement from military, 40, *40*
in ROTC, 7, 16, 18
as secretary of state, *4*, 4–5, *5*,
    8, *9*, 41–43, *42*
in South Korea, 31
thirteen rules followed by, 10
in Vietnam, *24*, 24–25, *26*
as Weinberger aide, 33

in West Germany, 21–22
as White House fellow,
    29–30, *30*
Yiddish spoken by, 15
as youth group leader, *9*, 41, *41*
Powell, Linda (daughter), 29, *29*, 33
Powell, Luther Theophilus (father),
    11, 11–12, 32
Powell, Marilyn (sister), 11, 12,
    14, 16
Powell, Michael (son), 29, *29*
Powell Doctrine, 38, 39, 43
Presidential Medal of Freedom, 43
President's Summit for America's
    Future, 40
Purple Heart, 25, 43

Reagan, Ronald, 32–33, 35, *36*, 39
Republican Party, 5, 6, 12, 39, 40
Reserve Officer Training Corps
    see ROTC
Rice, Condoleezza, *41*
Roosevelt, Franklin D., 12, 19
ROTC (Reserve Officer Training
    Corps), 7, 16, 18, *18*
Rumsfeld, Donald, 6, *41*

Saudi Arabia, 38
Schwarzkopf, H. Norman, 38
September 11, 2001 terrorist
    attacks, 6, 8
South Africa, *4*
South Korea, 31
Soviet Union, 21, *21*, 25, 37

Taliban, 8
Truman, Harry, 19, *19*
Tuskegee Airmen, 19, *19*

United Nations, 9, *9*, 38, 41–42

Vietnam War, 18, *24*, 24–28, *25*, *26*,
    27, *28*, 39

Weinberger, Caspar, 30, 33, 35,
    36, *36*
West Germany, *21*, 21–22
West Point (U.S. Military
    Academy), 19
World War II (1939-45), 12, 19, 21

Yiddish, 15

About the Author

Geoffrey M. Horn is a freelance writer and editor with a lifelong interest in politics and the arts. He is the author of books for young people and adults, and has contributed hundreds of articles to encyclopedias and other reference books, including *The World Almanac*. He graduated summa cum laude with a bachelor's degree in English literature from Columbia University, in New York City, and holds a master's degree with honors from St. John's College, Cambridge, England. He lives in southwestern Virginia, in the foothills of the Blue Ridge Mountains, with his wife, four cats (at last count), and one rambunctious collie. He dedicates this book to Alta Meeks and to the memory of Marie Brown.